AUSTRALIA'S *Fascinating Birds*

A PICTORIAL GUIDE BY DON GOODSIR AM
ILLUSTRATED BY TONY OLIVER & NICOLA ORAM

DEDICATION

This book is dedicated to my grandchildren Jasper, Merlene, Coen, Lance and Kada Hutt and to all young Australians who love and care for our country.

Acknowledgments

There are many people who gave me the opportunity to observe birds in the Australian bush and to enhance my understanding of them throughout my life. In particular, my parents Harry and Molly Goodsir and my grandparents Henry and Florence Moore of 'Glen Alvon', Westbrook Singleton. The Gould League of Bird Lovers, school teachers who inspired me with a love of Australia and a childhood friend and ornithologist Lawry Haines, have all nurtured my love and understanding of Australia's natural heritage. In particular my thanks go to Alan Morris, of the National Parks and Wildlife Service, who befriended me when living at Coonabarabran and has assisted with the accuracy of this text.

Other people along the way who have encouraged me include the late Alec Chisholm, Dr Vincent Serventy and my wife Julie, who has been of great help, not only with her bird watching and proof reading, but also with her encouragement and support.

FOREWORD

Most people are fascinated by birds. They are lively, colourful creatures that can be encountered almost everywhere. The presence of birds certainly brings colour and interest to our lives. Birds can signal the change of seasons or as in Noah's and Columbus' case, the welcome presence of land.

Birds have inspired poets throughout the ages and are the subject of Aboriginal legends. Rex Ingamells wrote of the Brolga legend in his poem "Bralgah"

Boolee, seeing Bralgah whirl,
thought the lithe-limbed dancing girl
was mocking him, and hissed a word
that changed her to a dancing bird.

(Land of the Rainbow Gold *Ed. Mildred Fowler Nelson 1967)*

Australian Birds attempts to further cultivate the latent interest we all have in birds, not only the more common and better-known Australian birds, but also those of special interest. There are more than 700 different bird species in Australia, 380 of which are found nowhere else in the world. Many species are rare or endangered, mostly through loss of habitat. Many of the birds selected for this book are likely to be seen where Australians live or travel, or are well known for their special characteristics.

The study of birds is a fascinating hobby. It is inexpensive, and can be enjoyed anywhere. There are many field guides now available to help with identification. Good binoculars, digital cameras and zoom lenses have brought a new dimension to bird watching. However it is best done by observing first hand in the field and making notes for future reference. Sir Joseph Banks, as he sailed up the East Coast with Captain James Cook in 1770, made the first record of our birds and wrote that they were rather shy.

John Gould is considered the "Father of Bird Study" in Australia. He visited Australia in 1838 and his books and illustrations, many painted by his wife Elizabeth, are highly valued and greatly appreciated today. The Gould League of Bird Lovers, founded in 1909, was an environmental education organisation named after him. Amateur bird watchers have been of considerable help in gathering valuable ornithological data.

Bird watching has its own rewards. It helps us connect with the land and as David Attenborough observed "I know of no pleasure deeper than that which comes from contemplating the natural world." If we wish to enjoy birds in the future, care must be taken to protect them and their habitats. Without birds, not only would life be less colourful, but a huge gap would be created in the balance of nature; insects would proliferate for a start. This potential danger could grow with global warming. It is hard to predict what changes will be made to plants and those creatures that depend on them. The consequences could be dire. However, as the good book says, "Don't worry about things - consider the birds of the fields..." Reflection helps put things into perspective.

The study of birds shows their uniqueness, our wonderful bird heritage, and the amazing ways they have adapted to their habitat. I trust that this book will encourage further study of our special feathered friends and the protection of our natural environment.

RAINBOW LORIKEET

Trichoglossus hematodus

These birds are pale green with a dark blue head, bright red bill, yellow-green collar and violet-blue abdomen. Painted all the colours of the rainbow, these lorikeets are beautiful and not bashful. They make sharp, continuous screeching sounds as they fly swiftly in flocks or in pairs and chatter noisily in high-pitched tones when they are feeding.

Rainbow Lorikeets feed greedily on blossoms, nectar and pollen. To help them gather pollen they have brushed shaped tongues, kept moist by a special fluid.

Rainbow Lorikeets are found along the eastern coast of Australia from Cape York Peninsula to Eyre Peninsula, as well as Tasmania, New Guinea and other Pacific Islands. They frequent flowering native trees in timbered country. Eucalypts, banksias and melaleucas provide the blossoms which form their main diet, but they also like insects and fruit found in orchards.

Blue Mountain Parrot is another name for this friendly bird. Like all parrots, it has special feet with two toes at the front and two more behind. The two forward toes enable it to hold food and bring it to the mouth.

'Budgerigar' is an Aboriginal word and means 'good bird'.

Wild budgerigars are green and yellow. Other colours such as yellow and blue are the result of careful breeding in captivity.

Wild budgerigars fly freely in densely packed, fast-wheeling flocks across the majority of inland Australia. Living in semi-arid woodlands and grasslands, these seed-eaters travel great distances in search of water. In times of drought they flock nearer coastal areas. After good rain they breed heavily and so the species survives.

In the early morning and late afternoon they fly to the waterholes to drink. But soon they are off again, wheeling through the air to another tree or landing on the ground in their search for grass seeds. In the heat of the day they rest in trees or bushes. One budgie by itself makes a loud and pleasant chatter. Hundreds of them perched together on their evening visit to a waterhole make an excited warbling.

BUDGERIGAR

Melopsittacus undulatus

EASTERN ROSELLA

Platycercus eximius

The Eastern Rosella is one of the best known, most colourful and commonest of all Australian broad-tailed parrots. It was first named 'rosehiller' because it was discovered by early white Australian settlers west of Sydney at Rosehill, now Parramatta. Over the years the name changed to 'rosella'.

As with all cockatoos and parrots, rosellas' beaks are so shaped that they can easily pick up seeds. They also like to eat blossoms, nectar, insects and fruit. Farmers don't like rosellas as they can eat their produce; however, they make up for this by eating the weed seeds, grubs and insects that can cause crops harm. You can attract rosellas to your garden by leaving out sunflower seeds.

Rosellas fly in pairs or small groups, close to the ground in fast, wavy movements. Before landing in a tree they glide upwards and fan out their broad, brilliantly coloured tails as they alight.

The Eastern Rosella differs from its Western Australian cousin the Western Rosella in, among other things, its colour and the way it flies. On thing that rosellas have in common is their very bright plumage.

The King-Parrot is worthy of this title. Although it is not as large as the Palm Cockatoo, the male King is rich crimson, green and black in colour, reminiscent of royalty. The green queen, or female King Parrot, is similar in colour to the male, but her head and neck are light green.

Worldwide there are over three hundred species of parrots. King-Parrots make a harsh screech, an occasional whistle and a short and a shrill "crassak-crassak". However despite their noisy calls and bright colours they are not always easy to see in the coastal forests that they inhabit.

All parrots have curved beaks for cracking open seeds and most of them have a crop like domestic poultry. A crop is a sac above the stomach used for storing food. They feed on fruits, berries, seeds and nuts. While orchardists are not fond of them, they are popular in gardens where they may eat sunflower seeds from feeding trays or even eat out of your hand.

Notice that two of their toes point forward and two backwards which helps them to climb along branches and hold food. It is also helpful for nesting in tree hollows often as deep down as 10 metres. It would be hard for both adults and young to scramble out if they did not have such feet. The young are born blind. The good news is that their numbers have increased and they are now moderately common.

Australian King-Parrot

Alisterus scapularis

Sulphur-crested Cockatoo
Cacatua galerita

Growing up to 50cm, this large and distinctive cockatoo is one of the most instantly recognisable of Australian birds. Entirely white, the cockatoo has a sulphur-yellow forward-facing crest, and a yellow wash under its wings and tail.

Cockatoos are very popular as pets and can be taught rudimentary speech. They also make excellent burglar alarms. However, their raucous screeching can be annoying, even in the bush where their calls can be heard throughout the day. Cockatoos are particularly noisy at dusk when they are roosting. Each flock has its own roosting site to which it returns after flying long distances to feeding grounds during the day. The birds squabble with one another as they jostle for positions in the roosting tree. In the morning the screeching starts again.

When the flock is feeding, a few birds perch in nearby trees in a well-established warning system. Should an intruder approach or danger be seen, these scouts, posted in trees as lookouts, give the alarm. 'Cockatoo' is an Australian slang expression for someone posted as a lookout.

As well as eating farmers' crops, such as wheat and oats, cockatoos like the seeds of grasses, herbs and weeds. They also eat insects and berries.

These parrots are pink-bodied and grey-winged, with a small white crest. They often fly in pairs or in large flocks of up to a thousand. Wheeling across the sky the flock changes colour as it changes direction, first showing the rosy breasts and then the grey backs. Rose-breasted Cockatoo is another name for these aerial acrobats. The name 'galah' was given to them by the Aborigines.

Farmers consider them a pest when they raid their crops, but also know that they help by eating the seeds of harmful weeds. Like most parrots, galahs gather ripened seed from the ground. When a large flock is feeding, one galah usually has its head up, looking out for danger so that it can give the alarm. Their usual cry is a shrill "chi-chi".

When the fledglings make their first flight, they sometimes fly as far as two kilometres. However, as they have not yet learned how to stop, crash landings are common. Many adult birds die from being hit by cars on country roads.

Because of their beauty and acrobatics, galahs are, unfortunately, popular as caged birds. If someone is called a 'galah', it is not for these reasons – galahs are also noted for their noisy chatter and mimicry.

GALAH

Eolophus (Cacatua) roseicapilla

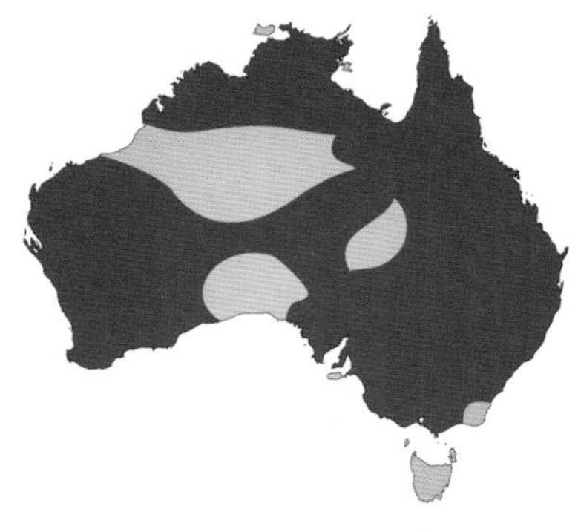

MASKED LAPWING

Vanellus miles

If ever a bird asks for trouble when nesting it is the lapwing, formerly known as the Spur-winged Plover! Breeding between June and October they give little attention to where on the ground they lay their three or four eggs. Nests are often just a small scrape in open paddocks surrounded by a few pebbles, grass, cow pats or twigs where the spotty dark olive eggs are well camouflaged. Horsemen riding by, or walkers who come too close to the nest, will soon know that they are in trouble. The adults will call out a long 'kekek kekek-kekekeke' or possibly a single 'kek' or two before swooping down to attack. A charge by a plover with its wings outstretched, exposing its yellow spurs, can be very intimidating. The Masked Lapwing's name derives from the black crown and yellow wattles on its head. Aborigines call them Jerry Jerries.

Both parents take it in turns to incubate the eggs. On hatching, the young move away from the nest within a few hours which is just as well as they have a struggle to survive. The chicks stay with their parents for many months even though they learn to fly within six or seven weeks. Once established, families of lapwings, make an attractive sight on golf courses, ovals, beaches and paddocks as they move about slowly and peacefully. A plaintive sound on a still, silent night in the bush is the distinct call of the plover carrying long distances across the paddocks. As they are protected birds they should not be harmed in any way.

Swallows catch all their food – small flying insects such as midges, small moths and flies – while on the wing and they often perform spectacular acrobatics as they twist and turn in search of food. They frequently flit low over water where many of their favourite insects are to be found. In some parts of the world the first swallow sightings are indications that warmer weather is on the way. However, in Australia not all swallows migrate to warmer parts; some spend the whole year in the same place. In Tasmania, most of them fly north to escape the cold winter and so Queensland has many more swallows in the winter months. Hundreds can be seen perched on overhead wires and fences. Perching on wire suits their tiny feet.

These small birds have a glossy blue-black upper which graduates to browner wings with a forked tail. Their face and throat are reddish brown with a white belly.

The Welcome Swallow is also called the House Swallow because it builds its mud nest under house eaves and roofs as well as under bridges and in mineshafts. European settlers have often destroyed places where birds build nests but, in the swallow's case, settlement has provided more safe sites for nests. As a result, swallows have increased in certain areas, bringing their sweet, twittering song.

Welcome Swallow

Hirundo neoxena

Nankeen Kestrel

Falco cenchroides

In open country, these small hawks can be seen hovering like helicopters as high as thirty metres in the air, searching for prey. A pale reddish-brown with grey tail, from below, when their wings are outstretched, the pale colouring of their underparts appears white. This helps to camouflage them as it makes them blend with the sky. Their food includes mice, small lizards and, sometimes, small birds. Like other members of the falcon family, they are also called sparrowhawks.

Although the kestrel does not fly as fast as other falcons it can hover over the one spot, its wings flapping only rarely, until it sights its prey. At times, especially on windy days, it appears to hang quite motionless in the air.

Kestrels do not build nests but use tree-hollows, nests deserted by other birds or chinks in rocks. Although up to five nestlings hatch, only the largest usually survive. These are the ones that hatch first and so get most of the food that the adults bring.

The Nankeen Kestrel is the most common bird of prey in southern Australia. As well as being found in open woodland and near farms in the country, it can be seen perched on tall trees, telegraph poles and buildings around cities and towns.

Nankeen is a pale buff cotton cloth from Nanking in China.

Sooty black with paler brown, the Wedge-tailed Eagle is the largest eagle in Australia. With wings up to two and a half metres across, these eagles can be seen, singly or in pairs, soaring high in the sky with their wedge-shaped tails spread out behind. Their wings flap only occasionally and so appear motionless as they circle, glide and soar. Often they climb to heights of 2,000 metres.

As it circles, the eagle looks out for prey. Once spotted, its victim has little chance as the eagle flies very swiftly and accurately. Its prey includes rabbits, young dingoes, birds, lizards and such marsupials as young kangaroos and wallabies. This predator also eats carrion such as dead cattle and lambs. Its sharp claws are well suited for tearing flesh and carrying food back to the nest to feed the young.

An eagle's nest consists of a large platform of sticks in a tall tree. From here, the adult can obtain a clear view of the surrounding country. The nest is lined with green leaves to keep it clean. One or two eggs are laid, but generally, if two eggs are hatched, only the stronger will survive. Both the male and the female, which is the larger, take it in turn to incubate the eggs and feed the chicks.

The Wedge-tailed Eagle appears on the badge of the New South Wales Police Force.

Wedge-tailed Eagle

Aquila audax

Boobook Owl

Ninox novaseelandie

At night the silence of the Australian bush is often disturbed by the call 'mopoke, mopoke'. Sometimes this sounds like 'boobook, boobook' and so the Aborigines named this owl after its hooting call, one of the most common calls in the Australian bush. It was probably a Boobook Owl referred to by C.J. Dennis in his poem Possum Park, where a mopoke call had scared boys walking across a park at night

"Mopoke! Who was that who spoke?

This is not a fitting time to make a silly joke."

The Boobook Owl should not be confused with the "mopoke", or Tawny Frogmouth.

The Boobook Owl is one of the smallest and most common of Australian owls. It can be found throughout the country including cities and towns. During the day this hawk-owl sits motionless with its eyes shut, among thick leaves or in dark places. It is camouflaged by its white-spotted brown feathers. Sometimes, during the day, the boobook owl is attacked by mobs of small birds. As dusk comes it begins to stir. Like most night animals, it has huge eyes to catch as much light as possible but, unlike most birds, owls have eyes in the front of their heads instead of at the sides. An owl's special neck allows it to turn so that it can see behind and then swing quickly back to the front.

The Boobook Owl has very sharp hearing and, around its eyes, special feathers which receive sounds and help it to locate its prey in the darkness. It flies silently, and so can surprise mice and rats as it strikes with deadly accuracy.

This well-known night bird is rarely seen because it is the best camouflaged bird in Australia. Frogmouths hunt at night but during the day sit motionless on tree branches looking like a dead branch or piece of bark. In the daytime their eyes are narrowed, hidden under bushy bristled eye brows but at night are wide-eyed. It is only when the bird opens its mouth to yawn that you realise that it has a large, gaping frog-like mouth. They do not get the prettiest bird award!

As it is a night feeder there is a common misconception that it is an owl. However a key difference is the feet – frogmouths have soft feet for perching, whereas owls have feathered legs with talons for hunting. Owls swoop down and pick up their prey with their feet while the frogmouths collect their food with their beaks. Insects and spiders are their most popular food, but ground dwellers, including mice and frogs, are also welcome. At night, Tawny Frogmouths sit still watching for movement. As they watch or glide silently they can easily detect their prey with their acute hearing and eyesight. Almost silent in flight, frogmouths easily navigate through trees because their huge eyes gather what light there is very efficiently, sharpening their eyesight.

Tawny Frogmouths live for at least 10 years and pair for life.

The Tawny Frogmouth call is a "oom,oom,oom" call repeated over and over again. People mix it up with the Mopoke call which is that of the Boobook Owl with a distinctive call of"boo-book" or "mopoke".

TAWNY FROGMOUTH

Podargus strigoides

Australian Raven

Corvus coronoides

If a flock of Australian Ravens is sighted in an open paddock, they have generally gathered to feast on a dead sheep or bullock. By eating carrion they help to get rid of blowflies and bacteria which would otherwise infest the dead animal. Ravens also eat young birds, lambs and insects and often forage for food in rubbish tips. Their black colour, their mournful 'ark, ark' cry and their habit of picking on weak and dying lambs often cause them to be considered evil.

I detest the Carrion Crow!

He's a raven, don't you know?

wrote C.J. Dennis. In fact, although they are alike, ravens and crows differ in some ways. The raven's feathers are entirely black while the base of the crow's feathers is white. Again, ravens are larger than crows and have different calls. When calling, a raven's throat hackles fan to form a sort of beard.

Because they can last for many days without water, ravens often survive in droughts when many other animals die.

The Magpie-lark lives almost anywhere where there is water, as it makes a special mud pie for its nest. The mud is strengthened with grasses making the nest look like a small pudding basin which is stuck to a tree limb, usually near its water source. It's not surprising then that they have been called Mudlarks. Four eggs are laid and it takes eighteen days for the eggs to hatch. The young Magpie-larks like puddling through mud in the shallow water of dams, ponds and rainwater pools, searching for pond snails although insects found on grassy areas are their main food.

The Magpie-lark is similar in colouring to the magpie but it is much smaller and has a finer beak. The adult male bird has white eyebrows while the female has a white forehead and throat but no white eyebrows.

Peewee and Peewit are other common names that are used. Its 'peewee' call is made when it lands and lifts open its wings. Like butcherbirds they often sing in pairs. When they take turns to sing in this way, as they sit on rooftops or telegraph poles, they are loudly proclaiming their territory to other birds.

MAGPIE-LARK

Grallina cyanoleuca

Australian Magpie

Gymnorhina tibicen

One of the pleasures of sleeping in the country is to be woken up by a chorus of magpies carolling melodiously. This joyful song, heard especially at dawn or dusk, has earned the magpie the reputation of being one of the finest songbirds in Australia.

However, during the breeding season between July and February they are likely to attack, swooping down from the sky like dive bombers if you venture near their nest or territory. They often use their songs to warn other groups of magpies to stay away from their territory.

Australian Magpies sometimes appear to be cheeky and inquisitive birds. They are common visitors to gardens and, if fed regularly, can be trained to perch on your shoulder and eat from your hand. They are very fond of raw meat.

Newly hatched magpies remain in the nest for about a month. For two months after that they still depend on the adults for their food. In early summer the young birds' plaintive cries for food are familiar sounds. These young birds grow almost as big as the adults while they are still being fed but they can easily be recognised by the light grey colour of their feathers.

Although there are several different types of magpies, with either black, white or grey backs, they all belong to the same species.

Currawongs are magnificent songbirds often heard calling 'curra-wong' at sundown. Other calls are 'caddow caddang' and a drawn out wolf whistle.

There are three species of currawong in Australia and at least one type is found in every state. The Grey Currawong is found right across all the southern states but the Black Currawong is only in Tasmania. All of them have bright yellow eyes and dark beaks which help to distinguish them from magpies and crows. Note the distinguishing white patch on the wing and white at the base and tip of the tail.

When breeding currawongs pair up and establish a territory in which they build a large untidy cup of sticks for a nest, well above the ground. The female incubates the three eggs while the male defends the nest and feeds his mate. The chicks are born blind and helpless and both parents help with the feeding, mostly rummaging for food on the ground.

Currawongs however are not as kind to other birds' young chicks! They prey on smaller birds and eat their young causing problems where currawongs have overrun other birds' territories. Imagine the terror they would create when a flock of up to 100 appears! Smaller birds such as wrens and pardalotes have disappeared from areas where currawongs have increased in numbers.

In the Sydney area this is quite a problem especially where the undergrowth of small bird's habitat has also been lost.

Pied Currawong

Strepera graculina

MISTLETOEBIRD

Diceum hirundinaceum

There are many different kinds of mistletoe plants growing in Australia. Some can be seen high up in gum trees. Being a parasite, mistletoe lives off other plants instead of growing in soil. Once the fledgling mistletoe birds leave the nest they live off large quantities of mistletoe berries for the rest of their days. The seeds, which are swallowed whole, take only twenty-five minutes to pass through the bird's body and, if they fall into a tree-branch, a new mistletoe plant grows. And so Mistletoebirds spread mistletoe plants throughout the country.

Mistletoebirds are small, colourful and common on mainland Australia. The males are glossy blue-black with a scarlet throat, and the females grey and white. However, they are rarely seen. As well as being shy, they usually fly rapidly, high up in branches, going from tree to tree in search of mistletoe berries. Despite their size their flight is fast because of their long, narrow wings. There are no Mistletoebirds, or mistletoe plants, in Tasmania.

The nest is one of the prettiest and neatest of any Australian bird. It is made from various kinds of soft plant material woven together with cobwebs and tied on to a thin branch. The inside is hollow with a slit-like side entrance. The two or three chicks poke their heads out from this as they wait to be fed. Both parents feed the young on insects.

What a distinct and far reaching call the Bell Miner has! Just as church bells carry long distances, so too does the 'tink tink' of this little bird, more popularly known as the Bellbird. It may be small in size but it has one of the best travelling calls of any bird as they are heard ringing out continuously almost over a kilometre away. What you hear are the notes of individual birds. They do not chime in unison.

Bellbirds are heard more often than seen. There are several reasons for this. They are small, olive green in colour and sit high in the canopy of trees where their voice carries well. They can be located but it may take some time to find them, even with binoculars. Both their call and their movement give them away. Their ring was the inspiration of Henry Kendall's poem 'Bellbirds':

It lives in the mountains where moss and the sedges

Touch with their beauty the banks and the ledges...

And softer than slumber and sweeter than singing

The notes of the Bellbirds go running and ringing.

The Bell Miner is in the same family as the Noisy Miner or Soldier Bird. However the Crested Bellbird belongs to a different family altogether and has a totally different call. The Crested Bellbird is also found in inland areas where the Aborigines called them Jumjums.

Bell Miner

Manorina melonophrys

The butcherbird is well named because it slaughters young birds to eat. Having robbed a nest of one or two nestlings, it hangs up its prey on a thornbush or wedges it in the fork of a tree. In this way, it can stand back and butcher its victim with its sharp, hooked bill. Other birds of prey, like the hawk, hold their victim down with their feet while tearing it up but the butcherbird's legs and feet are too small for it to be able to do this. By making a larder it ensures that it can come back at leisure for more food. The butcherbird also eats mice, lizards, insects and some fruit. If other birds intrude into its territory, the butcherbird frightens them off by snapping its bill.

Grey-backed with paler bellies, these birds are superb songsters and often sing duets. First one will sing and then stop. This will be followed by the whistling of a second songster.Then the first one starts again and the performance continues in this way with both birds standing straight and bowing low. In Tasmania, the butcherbird is known as the Whistling Jackass.

In some cases, young butcherbirds stay with their parents for over a year and help them feed the nestlings the following year.

GREY BUTCHERBIRD
Cracticus torquatus

SILVEREYE

Zosterops lateralis

These tiny birds, with the 'silver' circle of white feathers around their eyes, are mostly pale green with an occasional blue band. Each year, thousands of them migrate from Tasmania to the winter warmth of southern Queensland, a distance of more than 1500 kilometres.

Each pair of silvereyes breeds two or three times in the spring and summer season between August and February. Two or three young are hatched in each brood. As autumn approaches, hundreds of pairs gather together in great flocks for migration. This takes place mainly at night although they also drift while they are feeding during the day. Some fly northwards for warmth, some wander in different directions and some remain behind. Metal bands placed around silvereyes' legs have helped provide information about the migration patterns of these tiny perching birds. Ornithologists have also been able to establish by this method that some of these birds live for as long as ten years.

The silvereye can be a nuisance when it causes damage to soft fruit but it is helpful in destroying many harmful insects. This sprightly bird has a voice of silver; its sweet and melodious song can be heard as it flits among the blossoms and outer foliage of trees and bushes in its search for food.

Sharp beaked, long tailed rainbow bee-eater
Nests in banks burrowing deeper and deeper

Found throughout Australia (except Tasmania) this small but brilliantly coloured bird migrates north after the breeding season from September to March, often in the company of swallows. Some fly as far north as New Guinea, however their return is always welcome.

Apart from their bright colours and red eyes, they have a distinctive bold black line through their eye, looking like a continuation of their beak. Both male and female have two long streamers or tail feathers but the male's are longer. They fly quickly and skilfully, twisting and turning to catch their favourite food in flight. Once it is caught the bee-eaters speed off to a post or tree to eat their catch. A fast flying bee has no hope once sighted by a bee-eater. Other food such as wasps and dragonflies are also caught on the wing, often over water. The bee-eaters' musical trill is frequently called in flight.

Nesting in colonies they tunnel up to a metre through flat sandy ground or loamy river banks to a nesting chamber. Other birds in the communal group sometimes help with the tunnelling. They don't pause at the entrance to the nest when entering but dive straight in at speed. Three to seven translucent white eggs are laid at the end of the unlined tunnel. The eggs hatch within three weeks and the fledgling birds are gone from the nest by the time they are a month old.

Rainbow Bee-eater

Merops ornatus

BROWN FLYCATCHER

Microeca fascinans (leucophea)

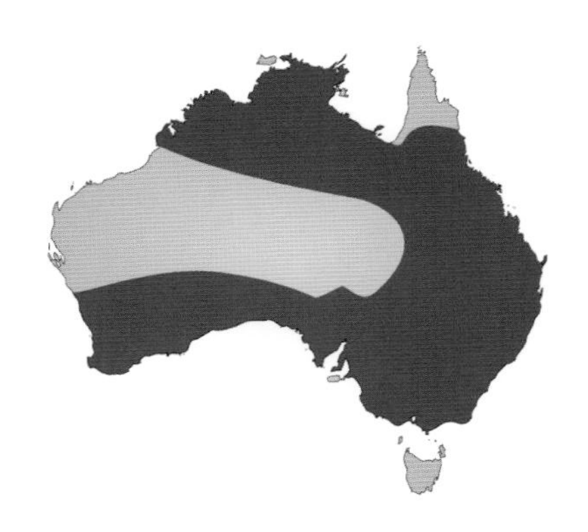

Peter-Peter, fencepost sitter,
Had a wife and could so keep her.
They built a small nest – not too swell,
And there he kept her very well.

The Brown Flycatcher, which most people call Jacky Winter, is also known as Peter-Peter because his song sounds just like that repeated over and over again. He likes to perch still on fenceposts and tree-stumps watching out for a feed. Because of this he is often called Post-sitter or Stump-bird. This relative of the Australian robins can spot the movement of insects from a long way off; he is quick to dash off to catch insects on the wing and then return to his perch to watch for more. Jacky Winter is an early bird out to catch a worm or grub, yet you can still see him perched late in the afternoon, on the lookout for a meal.

Both male and female adults help with the setting up of a home. Their nest is one of the smallest and most delicate of any birds. It is a fragile saucer of fine grass and hair bound with spider-webs and is built on an open branch. The male does keep his wife very well while she is brooding the eggs by bringing her plenty of food.

Although not very colourful, Jacky Winter is a fearless and friendly bird that can often be seen in gardens.

Wrens are tiny birds with long, cocked-up tails. With such tails it is no wonder they are poor fliers. Blue-coloured wrens are found all over Australia but the Superb Blue Wren is only common in eastern Australia. 'Superb' is certainly a suitable name for the male blue wren. Jenny Wren, however, is rather plain except for her orange-brown legs, beak and feathers around her eyes.

Blue wrens usually live in family groups. At first sight, a group might appear to have one male and many female wrens. This is because the younger males, which you can tell by their black beaks, only develop blue feather during the breeding season. Old males keep their blue breeding plumage.

All members of the family feed the nestlings for the first twelve to thirteen days after they hatch and before they leave the nest. In some seasons one pair may nest and raise three separate broods.

Blue wrens are lively, friendly birds that hop hurriedly about in their search for insects. They are often seen in gardens but do not like to venture far out into the open. The Superb Blue Wren is also known as the Superb Fairy-wren.

Superb Blue Wren

Malurus cyaneus

Yellow-tailed Thornbill

Acanthiza chrysorrhoa

Of all thornbills, the Yellow-tailed Thornbill is the easiest to recognise. It is generally seen in pairs or in flocks, hopping across the ground in search of insects. When it is disturbed, and flies off for a short distance, its yellow rump can be seen. Its bill, shaped like a thorn, is ideal for catching the insects and spiders that it eats.

It is also know as a Tomtit. For such a small bird, the Yellow-tailed Thornbill builds a surprisingly large nest; it has two storeys and is about the size and shape of a small football. It is made of grass and other plants bound together with cobwebs and has a side entrance in the lower part and an open, cup-shaped section at the top. Tomtits breed much earlier than most birds, often commencing in early winter. Their nests, however, are frequently attacked by butcherbirds and ravens.

Thornbills are a member of the warbler family and, of all thornbills, the yellow-tailed has the liveliest and loudest song. It is very common throughout most of Australia and does not appear to be afraid of humans.

Little Button-quail live on the ground. When disturbed in an open paddock they quickly rise in fright to escape. With a loud whirr of wings they fly furiously for a short distance just above the ground before dropping to the earth. They soon run off, and, being so well camouflaged, with speckled brownish plumage, quickly disappear. To find and flush them out again is almost impossible. They are also known as Swift-flying Quail.

The female button-quail is larger than the male and does all the courting. The male is left to sit on the nest and care for the four or five eggs that she lays. The nest is a small, grass-lined hollow in the ground. The chicks hatch after only two weeks and are then looked after by the father. Breeding takes place throughout the year, but especially after good rain. The button-quail population increases when there are plenty of grass seeds to eat; their beaks are well-suited to eating these. They enjoy insects as well. When a dry spell comes these game birds wander far and wide through grasslands in search of seeds.

Their enemies include such predators as cats, dogs, foxes, dingoes and man.

Little Button-quail

Turnix velox

What strong, powerful feet and claws these birds have! All the better to dig a large hole in the ground up to a metre deep. They then pile up a huge mound of leaf litter, soil and other plant material on top. Once rain has fallen to help rot all this material the female lays up to 30 eggs in the top section above ground level. These are laid during a period of several weeks. The mound heats up like an oven or giant compost heap to incubate the eggs. The male heaps a final layer of sand on the mound and takes charge. To ensure that the heat is kept at an even temperature of 33°C, he pushes in his beak, which acts like a thermometer, at various places around the mound. After testing the temperature he adjusts the mound if necessary.

Imagine the struggle the young chicks have after hatching as they scramble through the dark mound to daylight. This initial effort is good preparation for life as their parents do not look after them at all. Chicks immediately start running about feeding for themselves on insects, seeds and fallen fruit. The chicks can often fly the first day.

Malleefowl are ground-living birds and are found in dry scrubland. Mallee is an Aboriginal word for the eucalyptus trees that grow in dry country and the Malleefowl is called 'woggoon' by the Aborigines. To avoid attack by predators such as dingoes and foxes, they roost in trees at night. Another bird in Australia that uses the "compost heap" method for breeding is the Australian Brush-turkey.

MALLEEFOWL

Leipoa ocellata

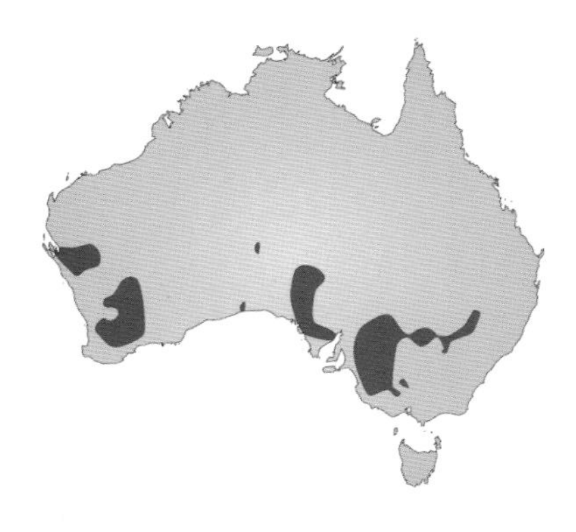

Australian Brush-turkey

Alectura lathami

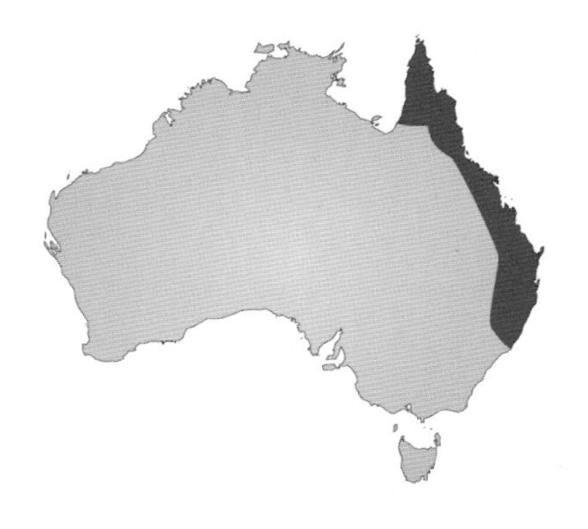

How would you like to be born in a centrally heated compost heap? If you see a mound of soil and leaf litter one and a half metres high and four metres in diameter in a rainforest or damp woodland, then you know an Australian Brush-turkey is close by. Low grunts are also a giveaway. Although they are quite tame at tourist sites, they will fly off in other places.

They scratch on the forest floor, building a giant compost heap for their nest. As the male scratches and builds he will open up the top of the pile when it rains to add more moisture to the mound. He does not want sticky beaks and chases all other turkeys away until the mound is finished to his satisfaction. This is when the nest temperature can be maintained at about 33°C.

Mating occurs on top of the mound. The female digs down until she finds the right temperature then lays her first egg. She may lay 10-20 eggs per season, in September and March. Most mounds hold no more than 10 eggs at any one time. The male may mate with another female at the same time. What an exciting time it is when after about 55 days incubating, ten young chicks start to scramble to the surface! They must "come up to scratch" otherwise they have no seeds or berries to eat.

The Australian Brush-turkey is one of three Australian birds that use their nest, and not their body heat, to warm their eggs. The other two species are the Malleefowl and the Orange-footed Scrub Fowl, which is found on the coast of northern Australia.

Did you know that Australia's smallest and most common finch helped save some of our early explorers from dying of thirst? Because Zebra Finches have a dry diet of grass seeds they must drink at least once every day. If they can, they will drink every hour. Explorers learned from Aborigines that by following flocks of Zebra Finches, which often number up to a hundred, they would soon be led to water. They had to be careful, however, as these birds sometimes drink saltwater. Like pigeons, they suck up water instead of scooping it up as most birds do.

They get the name 'zebra' from the black and white stripes on their tails and on the breasts of the males. As with many other birds, the male is more brightly coloured, with a blue head and chestnut flanks. The male's colouring explains, too, why Zebra Finches are called Chestnut-eared Finches.

In dry, inland country, Zebra Finches breed after rain when food becomes plentiful for the young. If enough grass seeds have not fallen to the ground, they pull the stems down to feed from them. Their nests, which are made from grasses, are dome-shaped with side entrances. They are usually built in low prickly bushes where they are safe from enemies.

These finches are popular in aviaries, where they are easily bred and studied.

ZEBRA FINCH

Teniopygia guttata

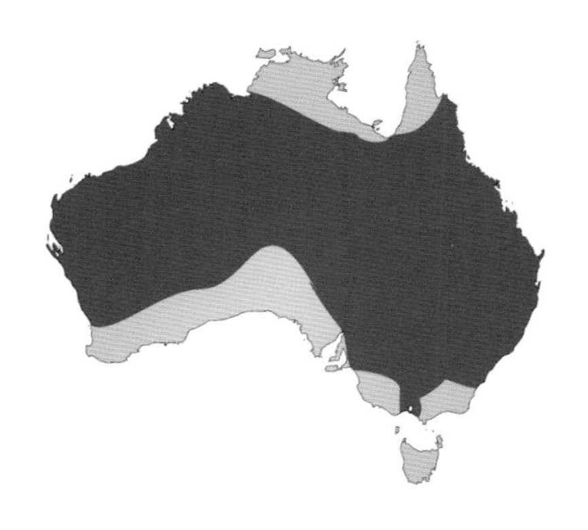

This bird was named after the famous pioneer, naturalist and artist John Gould. The educational organisation, The Gould League of Bird Lovers was also named after him when it was founded in Victoria in 1910.

This attractive finch is more likely to be seen in aviaries and zoos today than in the wild where its numbers have declined dramatically. Fire and land clearing have meant that many seed-producing plants have been lost. Disease and illegal trapping are other explanations. They are now uncommon even in the remote Kimberley region and Arnhem Land and their range of distribution has about halved since European settlement. Gouldian Finches are now seen in flocks of only up to a hundred or so whereas once they were seen in flocks of a thousand or more, especially around waterholes. So when you admire a Gouldian Finch bred in captivity think of what has happened to provide for your enjoyment.

During the mating season the male attracts a mate by puffing up his feathers, dancing and making special calls. Some males pick up a grass stem and wave it about to attract a female. Like all of the 20 or so native Australian finches the Gouldian Finch mates for life. Nests are usually built in small tree hollows with a small lining of grass. Finches sometimes breed twice a year with a clutch of 4-8 eggs if there is plenty of food and water. So with the birds' strong breeding instinct and our care for the environment there is hope for the future. Numbers may even increase!

GOULDIAN FINCH

Chloebia gouldiae

Scarlet Robin

Petroica multicolor

The Scarlet Robin is one of five Australian Robin Redbreasts. All of them are easily spotted because of their bright plumage. Notice, too, the Scarlet Robin's very distinct white cap.

You may have heard C.J. Dennis' rhyme:

Red robin, he's a perky chap, an' this was his refrain:

'Dear, it's a pity that poor Jenny is so plain.'

In spite of this, they make a loving couple and a good team. While the hen builds the nest, the cock feeds her. He continues feeding her while she is sitting on the eggs and for some time after the nestlings have hatched. Later, both adults help feed the young. The nest is a neat cup shape, made of fine pieces of soft bark and grasses which are bound together with cobwebs. It is built during spring and summer and is found high in tree-forks or in hollow stumps in highland forests and woodlands. Cuckoos sometimes lay their eggs in Scarlet Robin's nests.

In winter, Scarlet Robins move to the lowlands where the weather is warmer. Then they can be seen in more open cultivated farmlands and in gardens.

This friendly robin is found in wet areas of the east coast and mountains, and is also is known as the Yellow Robin, Southern Yellow Robin and Yellow Bob. Yellow Robins are flycatchers and do not seem to be afraid of humans at all. At times they become so curious that they will fly onto somebody's hat or shoulder. They have olive rumps and bright yellow bellies.

These bush songsters make the most of each day. Their 'choo choo' call can be heard before many of the other dawn singers and they are one of the last birds to roost at night. During the day they dart about the bush in their search for insects. You may see them perching sideways, close to the ground on tree trunks, ready to pounce on any ants that may be passing by. The shape of their beaks, like those of other robins and flycatchers, such as Willie Wagtail and Brown Flycatcher, enables them to catch flies easily.

EASTERN YELLOW ROBIN

Eopsaltria australis

New Holland Honeyeater

Phylidonyris novaehollandiae

Australia was once known as New Holland. This member of Australia's largest bird family was probably given its name because it is so common along the Australian coast. Perhaps 'New Pollen Honeyeater' would also be a suitable name; its beak is always brushing new pollen as it pries into blossoms in search of honey. Notice the slim downward curve of the beak which enables it to delve into native plants and suck out the honey with its brush-like tongue. Grevilleas, banksias and gum-trees provide its favourite nectar. These native plants are the best way to attract honeyeaters to your garden. As well as honey, these birds like to eat insects.

Most birds nest in spring and summer but the New Holland Honeyeater nests right throughout the year. It takes great care to find the best position. In summer it keeps cool by building its nest inside shrubs in the shade; in winter it catches the warmth of the sun by building on the outside of a bush or low tree on the northern side.

Not only is the Little Wattlebird the smallest of the wattlebirds, but also it is really an impostor. Wattlebirds get their name not from any connection with wattle trees, but from the strange pieces of flesh, known as 'wattles', that hang from below the eyes. Many birds, including farmyard fowls, have them. However, the Little Wattlebird has no wattles at all. Perhaps more suitable names by which it is known are Mock Wattlebird and Mock Gill-bird.

Like all honeyeaters, the Little Wattlebird is active and aggressive in its behaviour and frequents forests and heathland where plenty of nectar and pollen can be found. It feeds particularly on the nectar of banksias and will chase other honeyeaters away if they approach these flowers.

This small bird has a loud and raucous voice. When John Gould was studying and painting Australian birds in the 1830s, he was told by the Aborigines that the Little Wattlebird's call sounded like someone being sick.

Little Wattlebird

Anthochera lunulata

RED WATTLEBIRD
Anthochaera curanculata

We all know that yellow wattle is Australia's national flower so what is a red wattle? This songbird is named after the red flaps of skin that hang under their ears called wattles. Australian domestic poultry have wattles. Its other name is the Gill Bird although the Aboriginal name Tallarook might be less confusing. As their red wattles are not always easily seen, the Red Wattlebird can be confused with the Little Wattlebird and other honeyeaters. To help with identification look for a grey-brown body with prominent white cheeks, a pale underbelly and a long white-tipped tail.

Like all honeyeaters, the Red Wattlebird has a long brushy tongue to extract nectar from flowers. It angles and dangles itself around flowers to poke out its tongue into the flower. While gathering honey, honeyeaters unwittingly collect pollen. These 'blossom nomads' move from one native plant to another doing nature a great service by pollinating plants as they go. They particularly follow the honey flow from district to district, flying to the blossoms of eucalyptus trees as they flower.

Their song is a loud 'choc' which contrasts with their noisy squawking and aggressive behaviour, chasing away other birds that want to move into their territory. Everyone knows they are about when their 'choc jock-jock' call is heard.

As this honeyeater hovers in the air with wings beating, its long, spine-like bill probes deep into blossoms. With this curved bill, the Eastern Spinebill can reach the delicious nectar at the bottom of long, tube-shaped flowers; in this way it can obtain honey that other birds cannot reach. Nectar gives the Eastern Spinebill the energy it needs to fly vigorously. As it darts from blossom to blossom, its wings flash in such a way that they make a loud clapping sound. The Eastern Spinebill also catches insects while on the wing.

Eastern Spinebills are usually seen together in pairs along the eastern coast of Australia from Cooktown to the Flinders Ranges. They frequent open forests and heathlands but are also attracted to house gardens by both native plants and the blossoms of introduced flowers. Although very active, they are quite tame.

The Western Spinebill is a cousin which is found in Western Australia. Eastern and Western Spinebills are very similar and, in the way they hover, closely resemble the hummingbirds of America.

EASTERN SPINEBILL

Acanthorhynchus tenuirostris

Pallid Cuckoo

Cuculus pallidus

Like all cuckoos, the Pallid or Pale Cuckoo has some unusual nesting habits. Instead of building its own nest, it lays its eggs in another, smaller bird's nest. Mother cuckoo usually removes another egg from the nest before she flies away. This keeps the count of eggs correct. Then, when the young cuckoo hatches out, it gets rid of its rivals by pushing the other eggs or chicks from the nest.The foster-parents treat the young cuckoo as their own and are kept busy pushing food into its squawking beak. Bigger and bigger the chicks grows until, finally, it is much bigger than its foster parents. It is just as well there is only one to feed.

The cuckoo is a parasite. It is useful, though, because it destroys many insects, such as the hairy caterpillar, that few other birds eat. It has a beautiful call too. Up to fifteen notes are repeated over and over as it slowly calls up the scale. For this reason it is sometimes called the Scale-bird.

The Pallid Cuckoo migrates within Australia. After spending winter in the north and inland it returns in July and August, announcing with its song that spring is on the way. Harbinger of Spring is another name by which it is known.

This member of the honeyeater family has a raucous call, especially when there is a sign of danger. Perhaps early settlers thought it looked like a coalminer with its coal-black face and bright yellow eyepatches.

Noisy Miners are often called Soldier-birds or Snake-birds. They are as brave as soldiers when they boldly band together to batter enemies such as snakes and goannas. Some of their 'armies' or flocks can number up to several hundred. Dogs, cats and other birds are also chased by them. Soldier-birds have a secret weapon – they can fluff up feathers over their yellow eyepatches of bare skin to make them appear bigger and fiercer. In this way they often frighten away their enemies.

The Noisy Miner does not feed on as much honey as some other honeyeaters; it also eats insects, which it finds among blossoms and leaves as well as on the ground. Native berries and fruits form part of its diet, too.

Normally the Noisy Miner likes to live in open country. However, it often visits suburban gardens and sometimes even flies inside houses in search of bread and butter.

NOISY MINER
Manorina melanocephala

Indian Myna

Acridotheres tristis

A common urban bird, the Indian Myna, also known as the Common Myna, can frequently be seen sorting through the litter, chattering harshly as they investigate rubbish bins, empty lunch bags and gutters.

These comical characters were not to be found in Australia until after gold was discovered in the nineteenth century. In the 1860s they were bought into Australia from South-East Asia. They can now be seen and heard in many of our cities and towns, often in pairs or family groups. At sunset they become particularly noisy as large numbers gather together for the night.

Sometimes other Indian Mynas will stop to watch as their friends dance up and down. At other times two or three will gang up and attack another myna. Perhaps, because they live together in large numbers, they are working out the pecking order so that each one learns its place in the birds' community.

Like other introduced birds, Indian Mynas have caused problems for our native birds because they compete for their food and nesting sites. In many places they are considered a pest.

Satin Bowerbird

Ptilonorhynchus violaceus

If you are called a 'bowerbird' it means you like collecting old things thrown out by others. That is just what the male Satin Bowerbird does when he is courting.

The Satin Bowerbird is named for the glossy, lustrous dark-blue feathers of the male. The male bird builds his bower on the ground. First he makes a layer of thin sticks and twigs and, on top of this, builds two vertical parallel walls of fine sticks. The male bird paints the walls of this tunnel, using his beak. He makes a paste by munching up a mixture of charcoal, dust, dry bark and berries and dabs this on with his bill or with a wad of plant matter. It is because of its blue feathers and brilliant blue eyes that the satin bowerbird collects mainly blue objects. Blue feathers, flowers, berries, marble and scraps of plastic are all put into the bower.

The male is now ready to attract the female into his bower, which is used only for courting, dancing and mating. He prances around making strange movements and sounds, mimicking the sounds of other local birds. The female, which is less brilliantly coloured than the male, then lays two or three eggs in her nest. This is at some distance from the bower and is built in a tree fork or clump of mistletoe, three or four metres above the ground.

Willie Wagtails are very restless birds. Even when resting, these fantails sway their bodies continuously from side to side. But as they fly through the air catching flies and other insects in flight, they dart and flit about, changing direction suddenly, their black tails fanning from side to side. As well as catching insects, spiders and worms on the ground, they often search for food as they take rides on the backs of horses and cattle. As they ride along these birds continue to wag their tails. No wonder these members of the flycatcher family are called 'wagtails'.

Our Willie has an attractive whistling song that often sounds as though he's saying hurriedly 'sweet pretty creature'. It can be heard at night, especially on moonlit nights, as he flits about the garden in search of food. Because of his song he has also been called the Australian Nightingale.

When they are breeding, Willie Wagtails build small, neat, cup-shaped nests which are made of fine grasses bound with cobwebs. They are often found near or over water. The nest is so small that Willie's wagging tail can be seen sticking out over the edge.

WILLIE WAGTAIL
Rhipidura leucophrys

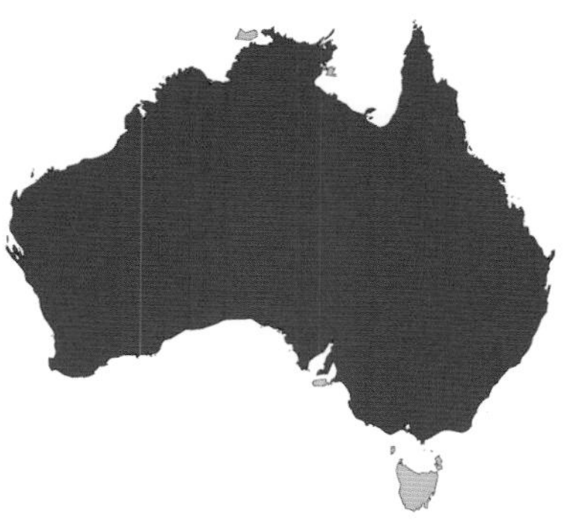

Laughing Kookaburra

Dacelo novaeguineae

The Aborigines thought that the kookaburras, with their heads and tails pointing to the sky, laughing heartily at dawn and dusk, were calling to the sky people to light up the sun. Early settlers called the Laughing Jackass their bushman's clock. In fact, the noisy cackle is used by a kookaburra family to let other birds know this is its territory and to warn them to keep out. Kookaburras live in large family groups and occupy the same territory for many years. They live for twenty years or more – longer than most birds.

Goldfish in garden ponds need to watch out as this largest of kingfishers is fond of them for dinner. Although kookaburras occasionally eat lizards and snakes, they feed mainly on insects. You can sometimes sneak close to a kookaburra as it sits, quiet and motionless, on a branch or post watching for its lunch to go by.

This iconic bird is native to most parts of Australia. However, they were introduced by early white settlers into Tasmania and Western Australia where they may have caused harm to other species by upsetting the balance of nature.

This solitary and beautiful kingfisher is familiar throughout Australia as it perches motionless on a stump or low branch looking for food. The Sacred Kingfisher's diet consists mainly of lizards and insects; it is only when it is near water along rivers, creeks and mangrove swamps that it fishes for small crabs, fish, tadpoles and frogs. It holds its prey in its long bill and beats it to death on a branch or stump before swallowing it whole.

When a Sacred Kingfisher attacks termites' nest in a tree, it is not looking for food but is burrowing to make its nest. It flies like a rocket at the termites' nest and, once a start has been made, digs with its bill and shovels the rubbish out with its feet until a chamber is formed. Nests are also made in earth banks and hollow tree limbs.

The Sacred Kingfisher is mainly seen alone except when it is breeding. Then both male and female help dig the nesting burrow, to incubate the eggs and to rear the young.

Although many Sacred Kingfishers remain permanently in Australia, others migrate to New Guinea and Indonesia.

Sacred Kingfisher

Todiramphus sanctus

SWAMPHEN

Porphyrio porphyrio

Swamphens can appear to be walking on water. As it moves though swamps, it spreads out its large feet so that the waterlily leaves support its weight. As well as being a good swimmer and a fast runner on land, the swamphen can also perch in trees.

The bright red shield on its forehead gives protection as it pushes its bill among the reeds and other swamp plants in search for food. Although it likes frogs and shellfish, it feeds mainly on tender, young reed stems which it bites off at the bottom with its strong bill. Like a cockatoo, the swamp hen uses its large foot as a hand to grip the reeds while it eats. Very few birds have a sense of smell; the swamphen does, and this helps it find its food.

Reeds, rushes and other plant material from swamps are used to make a platform for a nest in the swamp. When the chicks hatch they are dusky black and have yellow bills. Only hours after hatching they can run and feed themselves. Mother Swamphen guides them by jerking her tail up and down and showing her white under-tail as the chicks follow behind in line.

Cape Barren Geese get their name from Cape Barren Island in the Bass Strait. This island and surrounding areas were frequented by the early sealers who hunted geese and gathered their eggs for fresh food. Later they were shot by graziers as they competed with flocks of sheep for pasture. Before they were protected by law these large geese were hunted so extensively that they almost became extinct.

Although they feed in freshwater lakes, rivers and wetlands, they also feed in saltwater. Their beaks are short and tough and their feet are only partly webbed so they are often seen eating tough native grasses, herbs and shrubs on land as well as frogs, fish and other water plants and animals. Note the colours on their beak and the black spots on their wings.

Like all waterfowl these geese court in the water but are unusual in that they mate on land. They lay three to six eggs in their nest of sticks and grass on the ground lined with down. Down is both the soft fluffy feathers on chicks but also the inner layer of feathers under the thick layer of outer feathers on adult birds. This keeps the goslings warm and dry in water. Water birds also have a special oil producing gland that gives additional water proofing. Within hours after hatching the goslings follow their parents and are soon feeding with them. They need a good run before taking off but once air borne fly strongly and have been seen grazing in flocks up to 250 birds.

Cape Barren Goose

Cereopsis novaehollandiae

MAGPIE GOOSE

Anseranas semipalmata

Up north in tropical wetlands, this large black and white goose (pied in colour like magpies hence their name) is plentiful, especially during the wet season when food is abundant. Magpie Geese have semi-webbed toes that help them walk on land for grazing on grasses and crops. Visitors to Kakadu National Park can see them in large flocks wading through shallow lagoons during April to June in what the Aboriginals call the 'Banggerreng' or the 'Knock 'em Down Storm Season'. Magpie Geese are also resident in NSW from the Queensland border south to Newcastle and in the wetlands of north-west NSW but are present there in smaller numbers.

Nests are large floating platforms of grass and rushes built near the water's edge. Flocks of thousands make a spectacular sight as they feed, rest or fly up in the air in a cloud of black and white. Imagine the noise when they all start honking loudly together! At night they continue to be noisy as they roost in trees in their thousands.

Other unique features are their breeding habits. They breed in threes, one male and two females. Each female lays up to nine eggs. It's not surprising then that they all take turns in hatching up to 18 eggs in a nest. Rather than collecting food in their beaks to regurgitate it to their young, they snap off seed stalks and other plants, return to the nest and feed the goslings heads of seeds and other plants.

Ducklings can swim almost immediately after hatching. Seven or more ducklings, swimming in a line behind mother duck or father drake, look like a fleet of ships at sea. They swim along quickly with the help of their webbed feet and are soon taking food from the water. Their tails come up as their heads 'duck' under the water to forage for plant material and water insects.

The Pacific Black Duck is a very common Australian duck. It breeds wherever there is permanent water, and especially in deep freshwater swamps. Despite its name it is a greyish-brown colour, with a flash of green on its wings. The most important marking to look for is the dark line that goes from the bill, through the eye and beyond. This marking and the deep quacking sound it makes distinguish it from all other ducks.

The greatest danger that ducks face is the loss of their natural homes – the wetlands. The building of dams and drains has resulted in the loss of many of these areas. When inland flood swamps dry up, black ducks fly towards the coast, usually at night. All ducks are protected by law; hunters must obtain a special licence if they wish to shoot them.

Pacific Black Duck

Anas superciliosa

BROLGA

Grus rubicundus

The brolga is noted for its graceful dancing. Facing each other in lines, brolgas prance forward on their long, stilt-like legs, bobbing their heads and shaking their legs. Then they bounce back to their original position. Sometimes they leap high in the air, extend their wings and 'parachute' to earth as if in slow motion. From time to time they make wild, deep trumpeting calls.

These Australian cranes are also known as Native Companions. The Aborigines have a legend which explains why brolgas dance. Buralga was a famous dancer who would have nothing to do with an evil magician who loved her. He became so angry that he cast a spell and, with a whirlwind cloud of dust, changed her into a stately bird. Some Aborigines imitate the brolga's dance in corroborees.

Brolgas are found throughout most of northern Australia on plains, wetlands and swampy areas where they feed on swamp plants, frogs, reptiles and insects. They are also found on parts of the eastern mainland. These wading birds look beautiful in flight and flocks of many hundreds can be seen flying to great heights.

Some brolgas have been know to live for up to sixty years.

AUSTRALIAN BUSTARD

Ardeotis australis

Standing 1.15 metres, Australian Bustards are large, somewhat plain and heavy, weighing up to 18 kg. They move about slowly in a stately fashion stalking for food like plant material but also invertebrates, mammals, small reptiles and the eggs and young of other ground nesting birds. When frightened they often stand motionless or crouch making them an easy target for hunters. Therefore despite being shy and well disguised, the Australian Bustard is classified as "endangered". Unfortunately while they are a protected species this does not necessarily mean their habitat is protected too.

Yet they are like no other Australian bird! When the male is courting it turns into a weird-looking creature by blowing up its throat sac into a large distorted but spectacular shape. It lifts up its short tail and makes it into a fan, struts about and gives off roaring calls to attract a mate. What a show off! This ritual can go on all day and is an irresistible courtship device that just has to attract the curiosity and interest of a female.

No effort is made to make a nest as the one or two large brown eggs are laid on bare ground near a grass tussock or bush. The female incubates the eggs which take 20-25 days to hatch. The chicks are soon running around after hatching and can fly within five weeks. Fortunately the chicks blend in with the colour of the ground. They are usually guarded by the male but stay close to mum for several months.

The Australian White Ibis is also known as the Sacred Ibis from its association with ancient Egypt. It is one of three ibis species in Australia. The others are the Straw-necked Ibis, which has straw-like feathers protruding from its neck, and the Glossy Ibis, which is different in colour and more likely to be found inland.

All species have long curved beaks to poke around in shallow swampy areas, feeling for frogs, insects, snakes, snails, worms and crustaceans which make up their diet. Recently the White Ibis, with featherless heads of naked black skin, has come to urban areas like Sydney.

White Ibis are seen poking around in parks looking for scraps and checking out garbage bins. They can be quite cheeky and aggressive even to the point of snatching food from your hand. This is a far cry from their sacred status in ancient Egypt where they feature in ancient myths and hieroglyphics on the walls of pharaohs' tombs.

The males courting ritual is rather quaint. He establishes his territory, and defends it from other males in a noisy fashion. A female is enticed by his showy parade with a twig as a special offering. Does she twig to what is happening? This hard-headed male bird keeps giving her twigs which she uses to build the nest. At least they both share incubation and feeding duties. Their nest can be built in trees either over or near water.

Australian White Ibis

Threskiornis molucca

BLACK-NECKED STORK

Ephippiorhynchus asiaticus

The Jabiru, as it is commonly called, is Australia's only stork. The Aboriginal name, djabiru, is also the stork's name in South America. Its neck is not always black as you will notice – its feathers have iridescent colours that change from green to purple and blue. The young immature birds are brown and fawn in colour, but after about four years change to the beautiful adult colours as shown. The young often play by leaping into the air with great gusto. The huge adult however stalks in a stately style through the shallows of the swamps to spear a fish or small crustacean. Frogs, turtles, eels and snakes are also hunted. When stalking in water it often stretches out its wings to form a shield from the sun so it can see its prey. Its long legs enable it to travel far afield in its search for food.

Like the European stork they build a huge stick nest up to two metres in diameter high up in a tree, in or near water. Two to four eggs are laid and the young remain in the nest for up to 115 days. The males have brown eyes and the females yellow ones. They cannot call due to a muscle deficiency in their voice box but make up for this by occasional grunts and by snapping their massive bill to make a clacking sound.

The name Jabiru became well known when a uranium mine was built in northern Australia. It is now the Bowali Visitor Centre in Kakadu National Park. The stork is a bird of myth and legend associated with good fortune, the bringing of babies and was popularised in May Gibb's Bib and Bub stories.

COMB-CRESTED JACANA
Irediparra gallinacea

Can this Lily Trotter

Walk on water like St Peter?

From a distance Jacanas look as if they are walking on water but can they really do that? Of course not! On closer observation they are gingerly going from one lily leaf to the next spreading their weight on their large grotesque claws and toes. Note their long, lanky, splayed out legs, feet and toe-nails facilitating their steps on floating vegetation. Not surprisingly Jacanas are also called the Christbird.

As well as this ability to walk across plants without sinking, the Comb-crested Jacana stands out in wetlands because of its red fleshy forehead comb – hence its distinctive name. The comb bobs backwards and forwards as it goes.

Jacanas build flimsy nests on floating leaves in ponds and lagoons and lay very distinctive eggs with brown patterned markings. Should predators appear, the young dive into the water and hide among the lilies, sometimes just poking up their beaks to breathe. Chicks can stay under the water like this for up to an hour when threatened. Adult birds can move their eggs and chicks to a safer place by picking them up and carrying them under their wings which have spurs like plovers.

There are eight species of Jacana worldwide but the Comb-crested Jacana is the only one in Australia. Other species are found in tropical lagoons to the north in Indonesia, the Philippines, and in South America and Africa.

The White-faced Heron is often called the Blue Crane. However, the White-faced Heron is neither a crane nor blue in colour.

Herons can be seen in waterways, wading in shallow water looking for food. Their long, curved necks enable them suddenly to shoot their beaks forward to catch their prey. Fish, yabbies, frogs, freshwater snails, lizards and even other birds are all part of their diet. When flying, the heron does not stretch its neck out in front as most birds do, but keeps it close to its body. In flight, the wing beats are slow and heavy and the legs stretch out behind.

The White-faced Heron is very common throughout Australia and can be seen either alone or with a partner. Often it perches high in trees. Its nest, which is not always near water, is a platform of sticks placed in the branches of a tree.

WHITE-FACED HERON

Egretta (Ardea) novaehollandiae

Pied Oystercatcher

Haematopus longirostris

The high piping call of the oystercatcher can be heard above the roar of breakers on beaches. Like most waders the black and white, or Pied Oystercatcher, has long strong legs and unwebbed feet which make it easier for them to walk along sandy seashores searching for shellfish and crustaceans. Oystercatchers have long broad and powerful beaks which help them to crack bivalved molluscs and to turn over stones and debris as they forage for food in the intertidal zone. They largely feed on worms, shrimps, small fish and bivalved molluscs.

Their nest is not very comfortable – just a dip in the ground away from the shore in sand dunes and shell beds. Nests are lined with seaweed grass or broken shells and both parents take it in turns to incubate the eggs. The two or three brown spotty eggs resemble the colours of the young chicks that are downy with brown stripes. Perhaps because it is so uncomfortable they leave the nest within several days. Once hatched and with open eyes, the chicks are off searching for food. Oystercatchers defend their nests vigorously against intruders. Unfortunately the habitat of these shorebirds is threatened by the many Australians now living along the coastline and the popularity of off-road vehicles. Dogs, cats and rats are also a menace.

All oystercatchers, including the Sooty Oystercatcher, have a bright orange-red eye, beak and legs. They are shy birds, moving away as humans approach and are found on shorelines throughout the world except in the Polar Regions.

SHARP-TAILED SANDPIPER

Calidris acuminata

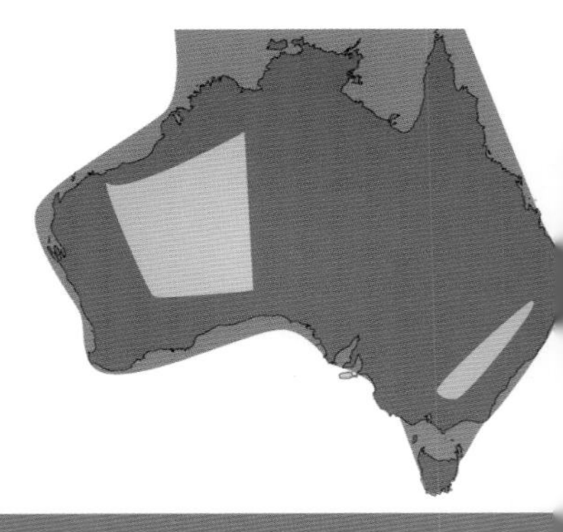

The Aborigines have a legend that the sandpiper is the spirit of a woman who many years ago lost her son. In summer when the sorrowful call of the bird is heard the Aborigines believe it is the spirit of the woman still looking for her son.

There are over 30 species of sandpipers in the world and fifteen of them migrate to Australia from Siberia to escape the harsh northern winters. Not surprisingly they are also called the Siberian Sandpiper, arriving in Australia in August and leaving in March. Imagine the effort and navigational skills needed to fly thousands of kilometres to get here from the artic tundra of Siberia! Other Artic birds such as the Golden Plover and Bar-tailed Godwit are also wading birds that have a similar migratory pattern. They are seen in their thousands on beaches around Broome in summer but some of our visiting waders travel as far south as Tasmania!

The Sharp-tailed Sandpiper is perhaps the most common of sandpipers - even more common than the Common Sandpiper. The sharp-tailed's bill is straight while some other small shorebirds have upward- or downward-curved bills. When in flight the distinct white stripe down each side of the dark tail of the Sharp-tailed Sandpiper helps accurate recognition.

Sandpipers like to forage in shallow water searching for invertebrates, insects and worms. Males and females are usually similar in colour and both parents take it in turns incubating the eggs. On hatching the young move away from the nest within a few hours. This helps them in the struggle to survive.

Pelicans take off very strangely, hopping across the water with both feet together until they are in flight. Once in the air they fly gracefully, often without flapping their wings, as they spot for fish. When they come down, their webbed feet come out together to break their landing.

Pelicans fish alone or in teams. A team of them will often form into a semi-circle, surround a number of fish and drive them into shallow water. They can scoop the fish into the skin bag under their bills. These bags can hold more than ten litres of water which drains out, leaving only the fish behind. As whole fish are swallowed, they can be seen bulging in the pelican's long neck.

Pelicans are amongst the largest of Australian birds and are found wherever there are large areas of either fresh or salt water. When inland waters dry up and there are no more shell-fish, fish or tadpoles, they have to fly off in search of new lakes and rivers. If the journey between feeding lakes is too long, they die.

Pelicans frequently sun themselves with their heads turned around facing its tail and their bills tucked down between the wing feathers along the middle of their backs. They then appear headless.

AUSTRALIAN PELICAN

Pelecanus conspicillatus

Black Swan

Cygnus atratus

West Australians are very proud of the Black Swan because it is their special bird. The capital city, Perth, is on the Swan River and the Black Swan is the State's emblem. However, Black Swans are found in all states of Australia.

During the breeding season pairs of swans stake out their territory like other birds, getting upset if other birds trespass and intrude. Swans defend their territory by making hissing and honking noises, fluffing out their feathers, raising their heads on their long necks and then dropping them in close to their bodies. When swimming along, black swans use these long necks to reach down under the water to feed on water plants and animals.

Flocks of swans, often in V-formation, make a graceful sight as they fly, with their necks outstretched, to new feeding grounds. They often make these flights on moonlit evenings when you may be able to hear their trumpet-like call and perhaps even see the white tips on their wings.

For part of each year – when they are losing their old wing feathers – swans cannot fly. It is during this moulting time that they can often be seen, in large flocks, on open lakes.

Professional fishermen keep a lookout for large flocks of Crested Terns with their black-crested crowns. A flock of terns hovering over the water and diving under the waves usually means that a shoal of fish is nearby. When resting, these birds float together in large 'rafts'. At night they fly to solid ground to roost.

They breed in large colonies on coastal islands. Usually, only one egg is laid – on the ground – and it is carefully rolled over from time to time to make sure it receives even warmth. This helps the embryo inside to develop properly. Nests are very close together, but just out of pecking distance from neighbours who carefully guard their territory.

This large, handsome bird is also known as Bass Strait Tern and Torres Strait Tern. In fact, some terns fly such great distances around the coast that they travel almost from one of these straits to the other. They live up to seventeen years, and are the most common terns in Australia.

Terns have webbed feet like seagulls but they are smaller and fly differently. As their flight resembles that of swifts and swallows they are also known as Swift Terns; and they do, in fact, 'turn swiftly'.

CRESTED TERN

Sterna bergii

AUSTRALASIAN GANNET

Morus serrator

This enormous and distinctive seabird can dive vertically into the sea from a great height to catch fish up to a depth of ten metres below the surface. What keen eyesight it must have to be able to spot its prey underwater from over fifteen metres in the air! With a wing span up to two metres, they wheel and dive in large flocks searching for shoals of fish below. Once located the swooping and chasing tires the fish and the birds are then ready to dive.

A gannet dives down folding in its wings before it enters the water. Its streamlined body then breaks through the water surface with neck outstretched, locates a fish and catches it in its dagger-shaped beak! To soften the impact on its head when hitting the water, air sacs under the skin and neck cushion the blow. Car air bags perform a similar job in accidents. It's not surprising that the Australian Navy's carrier-borne anti-submarine plane was called a Gannet.

The honking sound of large colonies of thousands of gannets in the breeding season is unimaginable. Nests are made of plant material and guano (bird droppings), which make the large breeding colonies quite smelly. Gannets fly out to sea for over 350 kilometres from the rookery in search of food. To land they fly into the wind, like an aeroplane, braking with wings and webbed feet outstretched. With such long return flights it's no wonder the adults take it in turns to brood and feed the young.

The Australasian Gannets are found in New Zealand and throughout the southern coasts of Australia and are similar to Boobies found in northern Australia. Gannets abound throughout the world and only fish in saltwater. A special gland above the eye sockets removes excess salt from its body.

These seagulls are found not only all around Australia's coastline, but on inland lakes as well. At sea, large groups float together in 'rafts' feeding on plankton which floats past. For an easy feed, they follow fishing trawlers returning to harbour.

When squally weather comes, thousands of gulls take shelter on land. They obtain food from city parks and rubbish dumps near the coast. By feeding on rubbish left by humans on beaches, seagulls perform a valuable cleaning service. They often visit airports too, where they can cause serious damage by flying into aircraft engines. In order to help reduce this danger, rubbish tips have been moved from near airports.

Silver Gulls generally nest in large colonies on islands off the coast. If chicks wander from their parents' territory too early, other gulls will attack and even kill them.

Young and adults gulls are different in appearance. The adults have white eyes with red eye-rings to match their red bills and legs; the young birds have dark eyes, bills and legs and no red eye-rings.

Silver Gulls live for up to ten years.

Silver Gull

Larus novaehollandiae

Short-tailed Shearwater

Puffinus tenuirostris

Imagine flying each autumn from the islands in Bass Strait, north across the equator to the oceans near Japan and Siberia, and spending the Australian winter in the warmth of the north pacific summer. If you were in a jet plane it would be an interesting return journey flying across to Alaska, south along the coast of Canada, then across the Pacific Ocean and back along the east coast of Australia to Bass Strait for the Australian summer.

Large flocks of Short-tailed Shearwaters fly this route every year, and without the aid of a compass. As food can be short and there are often storms, it is no wonder that some of these long-distance travellers are exhausted as they near home. Some die and are washed up along the Australian coast.

The way shearwaters fly may help to explain how they can migrate so far; they beat their wings rapidly, then glide stiff-winged and then flap them again as they fly onwards. Shearwaters return to the same nesting burrow every year. This burrow is in soft soil and is just one in a colony of many thousands.

Short-tailed Shearwaters are also called Muttonbirds. They are sought by man not only for eating but for their special oil. However, they are not an endangered species and are believed to be one of Australia's most numerous birds.

Down under the water it dives with its webbed feet moving strongly together. The cormorant can stay underwater for half a minute or more; its hooked beak is ideal for catching fish, crabs, and other marine life. On top of the water it swims in a more leisurely way, its feet moving one after the other, its eyes searching for signs of fish below. The cormorant will continue to fish until it has had enough for its daily meal.

Next it perches and stretches out its wings to dry. A special oil gland in its body oils the feathers and helps shed water. Unlike other waterbirds, the cormorant does not have waterproof wings. This helps it to fish; its wings and body become heavy with water and so it is easier for it to dive quickly under the water.

This cormorant breeds in colonies all the year round. It is usually found near the sea but sometimes visits inland lakes. It is called 'pied' because of its black and white colour.

Pied Cormorant

Phalancrocorax varius

EMU

Dromaius novaehollandiae

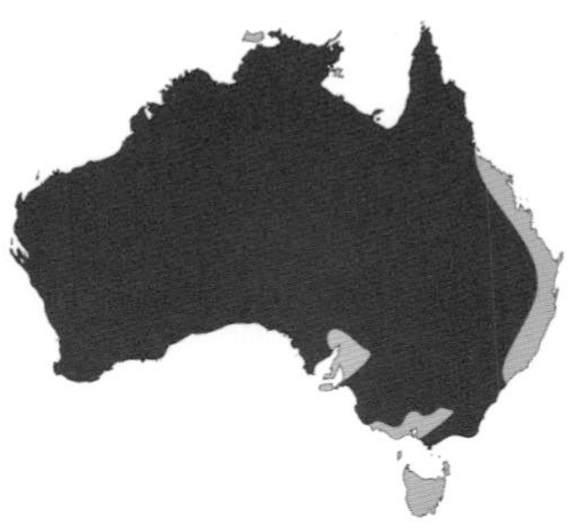

Standing up to two metres high, the emu is Australia's largest bird. It wanders over most parts of the Australian mainland feeding on grass, the flowers of native plants and insects. When chased, this well-camouflaged, flightless bird can run as fast as fifty kilometres an hour. It has a deep drumming voice.

The emu's egg weighs about the same as twelve hen eggs and has a hard, dark green shell. It needs to be tough as the nest is made of trampled grass and is often out in the open. The female lays from nine to twenty eggs at one time. She then wanders off and leaves the male to brood the eggs for about eight weeks. The new-born chicks have a colourful pattern of striped down. They can walk, run and feed immediately. Father looks after them for eighteen months, keeping them warm beneath his feathers at night. These feathers are very soft as the small vanes are not held together by barbs as are normal feathers. They are also unique in that they have two feathers coming out of the one base or quill. This double plume grows up to 45 cms, and bunches of them were worn with pride on the slouch hats of the Australian Light horsemen.

The emu, along with the kangaroo and wattle, can be seen on the Australian Coat of Arms.

The Superb Lyrebird is named for the Ancient Greek instrument, which its beautiful curved tail resembles. The tail of the adult male bird has a set of sixteen feathers and, when he is courting, he spreads it out and brings it forward over his head to cover his body like an open fan.

The superb lyrebird is a dancer, actor, singer and mimic. He usually performs on a large mound which he makes out of soil. Although he has a powerful call of his own, the male can imitate up to fifteen other birds. Sounds of dogs barking, gates closing or timber being sawn can also be imitated by this master mimic.

The female, too, is a mimic but her special task is to build the nest. This is a large dome of sticks, ferns and moss and is lined with feathers and moss. It is generally built on a rock, tree stump or tree roots. Only one egg is laid and it takes about six weeks to hatch out. Lyrebirds use their strong feet and claws to rake over the earth in their search for worms and insects. These shy birds are difficult to find in the ferny gullies they frequent. However, you can see the lyrebird's tail on any ten-cent coin.

Superb Lyrebird

Menura novaehollandiae

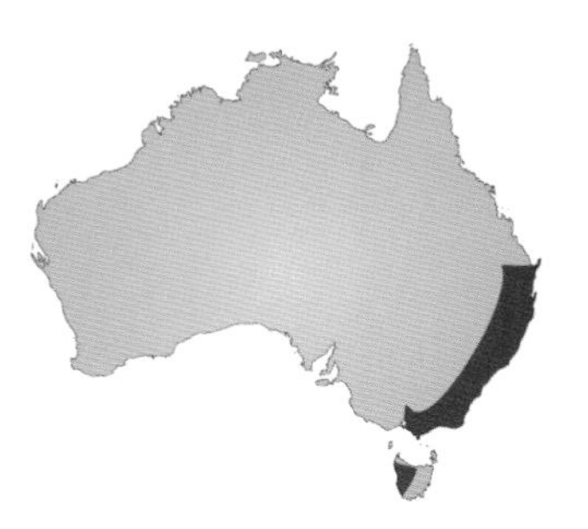

GREEN CATBIRD

Ailuroedus crassirostris

If you have not heard the catbird's call you are in for a surprise! The sound of meowing or screaming cats coming from tall rainforest trees is a very eerie and unusual sound indeed! The cry of the catbird may also sound like the cry of a small baby. An Aboriginal legend about them tells of a dying man, mortally wounded in battle, bewailing the fact that his tribe was burying him on the wrong mountain. He kept crying at each mountain top until the right peak was found.

These stocky birds are hard to locate because they are well camouflaged to blend with the green foliage of the rainforest. They eat a great variety of food – earthworms, lizards, buds, berries, bees and other insects. Figs are also a favourite part of their diet.

It is confusing that the Green Catbird is also called the Green Bowerbird. While it belongs to the bowerbird family it does not build a bower for courting purposes like the Satin Bowerbird, although these two species often are found in the same area. The male and female bond for life and the male maintains the relationship by feeding his mate throughout the year. Their nests are a deep bulky cup of vines and twigs in the crown of a tree or tree fern where two to three eggs are laid. Both sexes help to rear their young and sometimes sing duets. I wonder if there is such a creature as a green cat!

Index of Birds

AUSTRALIA'S *Fascinating Birds*

by Don Goodsir

ISBN 9781925367485		Qty
RRP	AU$26.99	.....
Postage within Australia	AU$5.00	.....
	TOTAL* $________	

* All prices include GST

Name: ____________________

Address: ____________________

____

Phone: ____________________

Email: ____________________

Payment: ❑ Money Order ❑ Cheque ❑ MasterCard ❑ Visa

Cardholder's Name: ____________________

Credit Card Number: ____________________

Signature: ____________________

Expiry Date: ____________________

Allow 7 days for delivery.

Payment to: Marzocco Consultancy (ABN 14 067 257 390)
PO Box 12544
A'Beckett Street, Melbourne, 8006
Victoria, Australia
admin@brolgapublishing.com.au

Be Published